People Who Help Us

Kath Cox and Pat Hughes

Notes for Parents and Teachers

This book provides a flexible teaching resource for Early Years history. Two levels of text are given – a simple version and a more advanced and extended level. The book can be used for:

♦ Early stage readers at Key Stage 1
♦ Older readers needing differentiated text
♦ Non-readers who can use the photos
♦ Extending skills of reading non-fiction
♦ Adults reading aloud to provide a model for non-fiction reading

By comparing photographs from the past and the present, children are able to develop skills of observation, ask questions and discuss ideas. They should begin by identifying the familiar in the modern photographs before moving on to the photographs from the past. The aim is to encourage children to make 'now' and 'then' comparisons.

The use of old photographs not only provides an exciting primary resource for history but, used alongside the modern photographs, aids the discussion of the development of photography. Modern photographs in black and white are included to encourage children to look more closely at the photographs and avoid seeing the past as 'black and white'. All the photographs were taken beyond the living memory of children and most have been selected from the Edwardian period between 1900–1920. A comprehensive information section for teachers, parents and other adults on pages 29–31 gives details of each of the old photographs, where known, and suggests points to explore and questions to ask children.

Editor: Vanessa Cummins
Designer: Michael Leaman
Photostylist: Zöe Hargreaves
Production Controller: Nancy Pitcher
Consultants: Suzanne Wenman and Peter Chrisp

Front cover: The main picture is of a children's ward in 1920. The modern photograph is of nurses and patients at the Royal Alexandra hospital in Brighton.
Endpapers: Photographers at work at a wedding in 1907.
Title page: Stribling & Sons Grocery shop c.1900.

Picture Acknowledgements:
The publishers would like to thank the following for allowing their pictures to be used in this book: Beamish, The North of England Open Air Museum 15, 19; Crown Copyright 9; Mary Evans Picture Library **main cover picture**, title page, 7, 25; Greater London Council 5; Hulton Deutsch 23; The Rural History Centre, University of Reading 11; The Royal Photographic Society, Bath, endpapers, contents page, 13, 17; Topham 27; The Wellcome Institute 21. All other pictures are from the Wayland Picture Library. All artwork is by Barbara Loftus.

First published in Great Britain in 1995 by Wayland (Publishers) Ltd
Reprinted in 2000 by Hodder Wayland,
an imprint of Hodder Children's Books

© Hodder Wayland 1995

British Library Cataloguing in Publication Data
Cox, Kath
People Who Help Us. – (History from Photographs Series)
I. Title II. Hughes, Pat III. Series 331.71

ISBN 0-7502-2122-4 PAPERBACK

Typeset in the UK by Michael Leaman Design Partnership
Printed and bound in Italy by G. Canale & C. S.p.A.

· Contents ·

A Brownie box camera and case, 1900.

Some of the more difficult words appear in the text in **bold**.
These words are explained in the picture glossary on page 28.
The pictures will help you to understand the entries more easily.

Mrs Reed is a teacher.

There are fewer than thirty pupils in her class.
Pupils ask questions and talk to Mrs Reed about their work.
The pupils do different activities at each of the tables.

This teacher is walking around the classroom looking at the children's work.

There were fifty pupils in this class.

Pupils sat in rows and had to work in silence.

The pupils all did the same activity together.

Miss Dunn is a cleaner at the shopping centre.

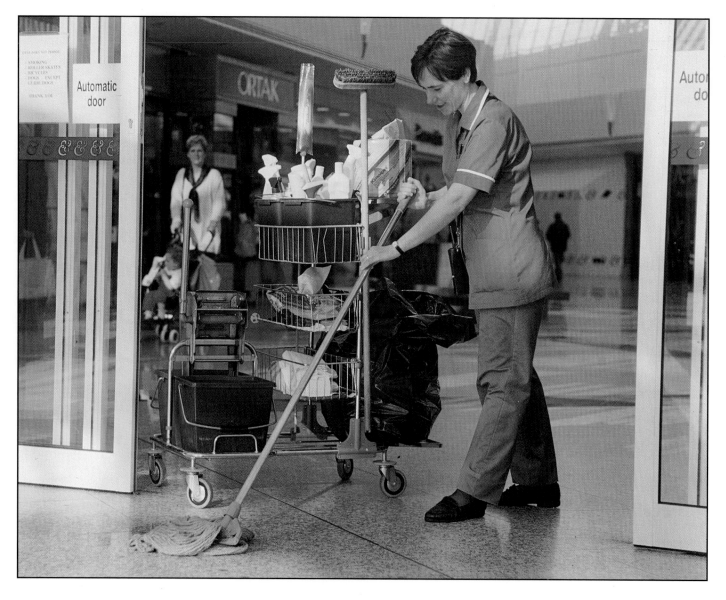

She works early in the morning or late at night when the shop is closed.
There is no carpet on the floor so Miss Dunn is using a mop.
She has a special trolley to hold her cleaning equipment.

This shop is being cleaned by men wearing smart uniforms and hats.

The men are using special machines to clean the carpet.
The machines are called vacuum cleaners.
Few people used vacuum cleaners in 1910 because they
were large and very expensive to buy.

Mrs Brown is a postal worker.

She delivers letters and parcels to homes and offices.
She is wearing a **uniform** and comfortable training shoes.
Postal workers drive vans when they deliver letters and parcels
over long distances.

Letters were delivered by postmen.

Postmen wore uniforms with a cap and badge and strong walking boots.
They had to walk a long way to deliver letters.
Some postmen rode bicycles to deliver letters more quickly.

Mr Grayer delivers milk on a milk float.

Milkmen and women bring milk to our houses in the morning.
The milk comes in glass bottles.
Milkmen deliver bread, yoghurt and orange juice as well as milk.

This milkman delivered milk on a milk cart.

The milkman poured the milk into bottles and small tins from a **churn**.
Customers paid the milkman who put the money
in a bag around his neck.
The milkman sold only milk.

Mr Brett and Mr McDowell are **refuse** workers.

Refuse workers take away rubbish from our homes.
They empty **dustbins** and throw the bags of rubbish into the back of
the lorry. The lorry carries the rubbish to a dump.

Refuse workers collected rubbish in a dustcart pulled by a horse.

Refuse workers emptied the dustbins from homes into the dustcart.
They also swept the streets with brushes.
Some rubbish, such as metal objects or cloth, was taken away to
be sold. Other rubbish was burnt.

Mrs Smith works on the **check-out** in a supermarket.

Customers bring their groceries to the check-out.
Mrs Smith adds up the prices on the **till** and waits to be paid.
Then the customers pack the food into bags ready to take home.

These assistants
are working in
a grocer's shop.

Customers told the shop
assistant what they wanted
to buy. The shop assistant
found the goods, weighed
them and wrapped them
up. Sometimes customers
paid the shop assistant for
their shopping at the end
of the month.

Mr Butler is a food server in a take-away.

Chilliburger..........135
Original or Garlic.......135
Allstar or 1000 Island....150
Bluecheese or Hawaiian..155
Baconburger + Cheese....175
Doubles Add to the Prices above........+ 74
Veggie Burger..........125
Vegetarian Samwich....100
Chicken Samwich......164
Fries Regular and Large..........55/70

Coffee....43/58 Tea 35/48
Hot Apple Pie 52
Special Value Meals
Burger + Regular Fries & Drink
Lunch Time Special 215 235
Veggie Meal........215 235
Allstar Meal......245 265
Sams Feast.........265 285
Chicken Meal......265 285
Children's Meal 215 215

CHICKEN MEAL

SAMS FEAST

Meals as shown   265

A take-away is a **restaurant** where food is served very quickly. Customers look at the board and decide what they want to eat. This take-away serves burgers and chips.

This is a take-away at a racecourse.

Customers enjoyed being outdoors watching the horse races.

The customers stood at the counter to eat.

This take-away served tea and buns.

Mrs Fox works in a **library**.
She is a librarian.

Librarians help people to find books, videos, tapes and maps to borrow. All the books are listed on the computer. Librarians stamp the books with a date when the books must be returned.

This man is a librarian.

The library kept only books and maps.
People asked the librarian for a book and he went to fetch it.
The books were listed on cards. The librarian stamped the cards with
a date when the books must be returned.

Dr Platt is examining a child in a hospital.

Doctors examine patients who are sick.
They use special equipment to find out what is wrong.
They write **prescriptions** for medicine to help make people feel better.

Dr Hood worked in a hospital in London.

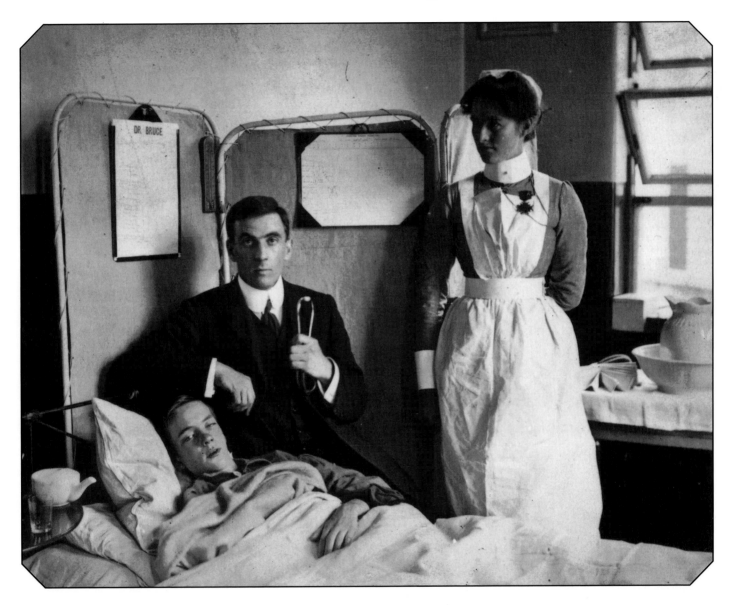

People had to pay to stay in hospital when they were ill.
Doctors had less special equipment to examine their patients.
Almost all doctors were men.

Mandy, Ann and Lucy are nurses working on the **children's ward**.

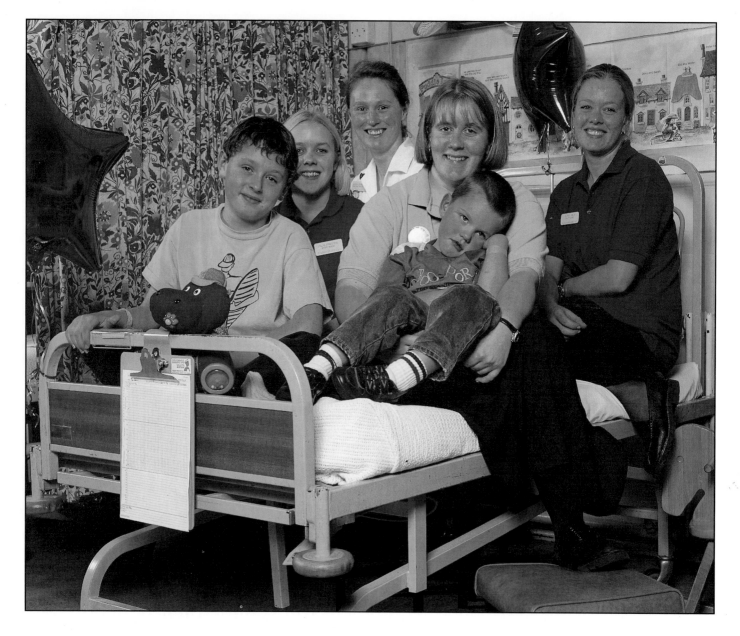

Nurses look after sick people in hospitals.
Some nurses work in clinics or visit patients at home.
Today, men and women train to be nurses.

These nurses looked after sick children in hospital.

Nurses wore long white aprons, collars and stiff cuffs on their sleeves.
The children had lots of toys because it was Christmas-time.
Only women were nurses.

This is police constable Jefferies.

Some police officers ride motor bikes when they are on patrol.
They can travel very quickly to a **traffic** jam or road accident.
They wear special clothes and a crash helmet to protect them.

This police officer is directing traffic.

Most police officers walked on their patrol. This police officer wore a special band on his arm to show he was directing traffic. There were no **traffic lights** in the streets. Only men were police officers in 1908.

David, Vicky and Tony are fire-fighters.

Fire-fighters wear special clothes to protect them from fire.

There is a siren on the top of the fire engine.

Today, there are women fire-fighters as well as men.

These men were fire-fighters.

Fire-fighters wore smart uniforms with
metal helmets and heavy boots.
There was a bell on the front of the fire-engine.
There were no women fire-fighters.

· Picture Glossary ·

 **check-out** A desk where customers pay for their shopping.

 **refuse** Things that people throw away.

 **children's ward** The part of a hospital where sick children are nursed.

 **restaurant** A place where food and drink is prepared and served to customers.

 **churn** A large metal container used to hold milk.

 **till** A machine used in shops for adding up prices and keeping money safe.

 **dustbin** A container used to hold rubbish.

 **traffic** Cars, vans, lorries and other vehicles on the road.

 **library** A place where lots of information is kept for people to use or borrow.

 **traffic lights** The red, amber and green lights that tell drivers when to stop and go.

 **prescription** A piece of paper on which the doctor names the medicine that the patient needs.

 **uniform** Special clothes worn to show what job a person does.

· Books to Read ·

Cleaning by G. Tanner and T. Wood (History Mysteries series, A& C Black, 1994).
Edwardian Britain by Michael Rawcliffe (Finding Out About series, Batsford, 1989).
Getting Better by G. Tanner and T. Wood (History Mysteries series, A & C Black, 1994).
Our Health, by S. Ross (Starting History series, Wayland, 1992).
Our Schools by S. Ross (Starting History series, Wayland, 1992).
Rubbish by G. Tanner (Turn of the Century series, A & C Black, 1991).
School Day by M. Stoppleman (Turn of the Century series, A & C Black, 1990).
Shopping for Food, by R. Thomson (Changing Times series, Franklin Watts, 1992).

· Places to Visit ·

Many local museums have small collections or displays about workers in history.
It is worth contacting them to see what they can offer.
The following examples are specialist museums.

Greater Manchester Police Museum
Newton Street
Manchester M1 1ES

   Telephone: 0161 856 3287

North of England Open Air Museum
Beamish
County Durham DH9 ORG

   Telephone: 01207 231811

Queen Alexandra's Royal
Army Nursing Corps Museum
Regimental Headquarters
QARANC, Royal Pavilion
Farnborough Road, Aldershot,
Hampshire GU11 1PZ

   Telephone: 01252 24431

The Ulster Folk and Transport Museum
153 Bangor Road, Cultra
Holywood BT18 OEU
Northern Ireland

   Telephone: 01232 428428
   Education Officer: Deirdre Brown

People's Palace Museum
Glasgow Green
Glasgow G40 1AT

   Telephone: 01252 24431

National Postal Museum
King Edward Building
King Edward Street
London EC1A 1LP

   Telephone: 0171 239 5420
   Education Officer: Barry Tennant

Further Information about the Photographs

PHOTOGRAPH ON PAGE 5

Hugh Myddleton School, London, 1906.

About this photograph

Education for most children at this time involved the development of basic levels of literacy and numeracy – these children are doing handwriting practice. The notions that teachers should educate the whole child as an individual or that children could enjoy learning were yet to permeate the classroom.

Questions to ask

How was the classroom lit?
Are the children enjoying their lesson?
What do you think the pupils are learning? Why?

Points to explore

Pupils – ages, physical appearance, clothes.
Teacher – age, hairstyle, clothes.
Classroom – layout, furniture, children's drawings, lighting.

PHOTOGRAPH ON PAGE 7

Cleaners vacuuming in a clothes shop, 1910.

About this photograph

The photograph comes from an advertising brochure produced by a vacuum cleaner company. The uniforms worn by the men could mean that they were employed by the company. Before vacuum cleaners, carpets and rugs were not fitted and had to be cleaned by hanging them outside and beating them with a stick.

Questions to ask

Do you think this was an expensive shop to buy clothes in?
How are the vacuums different from modern vacuums?
Why are the shop assistants watching the cleaners?

Points to explore

Cleaners – age, gender, clothes, equipment.
Background – people, fittings, furniture, glass cases, plants.

PHOTOGRAPH ON PAGE 9

A postal worker, 1900.

About this photograph

By 1900 even the most remote villages had a regular postal delivery. Most letters were delivered on foot and postmen received a boot allowance in recognition of this fact. In 1897 the Post Office experimented with early petrol and steam driven vans to deliver parcels. However it was not until 1919 that the Post Office established its own fleet of vans.

Questions to ask

What kind of house is this and where is it located?
Where are the letters carried?
Why is the postman wearing a uniform?

Points to explore

Postal worker – gender, age, uniform.
Background – building, people.

PHOTOGRAPH ON PAGE 11

Milkman and his assistant, London, 1908.

About this photograph

People in the countryside would buy their milk direct from the farmer. In the towns the milkman was a familiar sight. Sometimes customers brought their own containers to be filled with milk. The prevalence of rickets amongst children at this time suggests that for many of them milk was not a regular part of their diet.

Questions to ask

What is the name of the farm that the milk came from?
What kind of vehicle is used to deliver milk?
Why are the man and boy carrying buckets?

Points to explore

People – age, gender, clothes.
Vehicles – power, equipment.
Background – buildings, street furniture.

PHOTOGRAPH ON PAGE 13

Roadsweepers, possibly in Bath, 1914.

About this photograph

From 1875 all town councils had to provide regular road sweeping and rubbish collections. Rubbish was collected by the refuse workers and put on carts to be taken back to the local dustyard where it was sorted. Any useful items were salvaged and sold to finance the collection service. Most Victorian/Edwardian rubbish was ash, soot from coal fires and animal dung. The soot was recycled to make bricks and the animal dung used as fertilizer.

Questions to ask

What kind of horse pulled the cart?
Do the people know the photograph is being taken?

Points to explore

Refuse collectors – number, age, gender, clothing.
Dustcart – size, shape, design, hygiene.

PHOTOGRAPH ON PAGE 15

Shop assistants in a grocer's shop in the early 1900s.

About this photograph

For most families shopping for food would be carried out on a daily basis particularly for perishable goods. There were no fridges and methods of preserving food were limited. Shopping would require visits to several shops, each specializing in certain produce e.g. fishmonger, greengrocer, baker. Notice the 'cash railway' system where money was transported in capsules on overhead wires to a central finance office.

Questions to ask

What are the shop assistants wearing?
Why is there a chair in the shop?

Points to explore

People – age, gender, clothing.
Shop – goods, packaging, furniture, overhead wire, lighting.

Serving food at the Epsom Derby, 1914.

About this photograph
The Epsom Derby has always been a popular event for racegoers. Temporary food stalls were common. The take-away van used gas canisters to cook by and heat water for tea and coffee. There were also ice cream stands, usually run by Italians.

Questions to ask
How is the vehicle driven?
What is being cooked?
How is the food served?

Points to explore
Food servers – age, gender, uniform, duties.
Customers – age, gender, clothing.
Background – litter, furniture, fittings, decoration.

A Librarian, c.1900.

About this photograph
Until the late nineteenth century most libraries were attached to universities and educational establishments or were private collections belonging to important families. It was only with the increasing literacy of the population that the notion of a public lending library came into existence. Notice that the librarian and the books are fenced off from the public area. People worried about theft and before electronic alarms it would be easy to steal books.

Questions to ask
What is the librarian doing?
How were the books catalogued?

Points to explore
Librarian – clothes, appearance.
Library – accessibility, technology, reading desk, shelves.

Dr Hood with a patient and nurse, c.1914.

About this photograph
The medical examinations of army volunteers during the Boer War had provided overwhelming evidence of the poor state of health of much of the population. Without antibiotics many of the diseases that we can cure nowadays could not be treated. Dr Basil Hood (1876-1978) campaigned for a free national health service. He was well-known for treating poor people at St Bartholomew's Hospital in London.

Questions to ask
What is pinned to the nurse's apron?
How ill do you think the patient is? Why?

Points to explore
Doctor – age, gender, clothing, equipment
Background – children, room, equipment.

Christmas at Great Ormond Street Hospital, 1913.

About this photograph
Nursing was an acceptable occupation for young women from wealthy families and required a period of training. Nursing care was relatively expensive so poor people turned to their family rather than professional nurses to provide primary health care.

Questions to ask
Do you think the uniforms were useful for the nurses' work?
What do you think is the matter with these children?
Why are there lots of toys?

Points to explore
Nurses – age, gender, different roles, uniforms.
Children – age, appearance, clothing, toys.
Background – furniture, equipment, decoration.

A London 'Bobby' on traffic duty, c.1908.

About this photograph
Police officers worked a seven-day week and very long hours. At the start of each shift policemen would march along the street together until they reached their 'beat'. Here they would leave the rest to patrol their own area and meet up with the sergeant at regular intervals. There were no official meal breaks. Policing was becoming more scientific and all police forces were using fingerprinting by 1907.

Questions to ask
Why is he wearing a uniform?

Points to explore
Police officer – age, gender, different duties, uniform, headgear.
Background – vehicles, buildings, road, street furniture.

London's first self-propelled steam fire appliance, 1900.

About this photograph
This was the first and only steam-powered fire-engine in London known as the 'Fire King'. Prior to this, fire appliances would have been pulled by horses. The design of the uniform was basically very similiar to today's – but with differences in materials. There were no female fire-fighters until 1976.

Questions to ask
What are the differences in the fire-fighters' helmets?
What equipment do the fire-fighters have to help put out the fire?

Points to explore
Fire-fighters – age, gender, uniform, headgear, equipment.
Fire-engine – size, shape, steering, power source, speed, lights, warning equipment, fire-fighting apparatus.
Background – buildings, road.

· Index ·

(Items that appear in the text)